MARCHA CRIANÇA

5º ANO
ENSINO FUNDAMENTAL

LÍNGUA INGLESA

Eliete Canesi Morino

Graduada pela Pontifícia Universidade Católica de São Paulo (PUC-SP)
em Língua e Literatura Inglesa e Tradução e Interpretação.
Especialização em Língua Inglesa pela International Bell School of London.
Pós-graduada em Metodologia da Língua Inglesa pela Faculdade de Tecnologia e Ciência.
Atuou como professora na rede particular de ensino e em projetos comunitários.

Rita Brugin de Faria

Graduada pela Faculdade de Arte Santa Marcelina
e pela Faculdade Paulista de Arte.
Especialização em Língua Inglesa pela International Bell School of London.
Pós-graduada em Metodologia da Língua Inglesa pela Faculdade de Tecnologia e Ciência.
Especialista em alfabetização, atuou como professora e coordenadora
pedagógica nas redes pública e particular de ensino.

editora scipione

editora scipione

Presidência: Mario Ghio Júnior

Direção editorial: Lidiane Vivaldini Olo

Gerência editorial: Viviane Carpegiani

Gestão de área: Tatiany Renó

Edição: Mariangela Secco (coord.), Ana Lucia Militello

Planejamento e controle de produção: Flávio Matuguma, Juliana Batista, Felipe Nogueira e Juliana Gonçalves

Revisão: Kátia Scaff Marques (coord.), Brenda T. M. Morais, Claudia Virgilio, Daniela Lima, Malvina Tomáz e Ricardo Miyake

Arte: André Gomes Vitale (ger.), Catherine Saori Ishihara (coord.), Christine Getschko (edição de arte)

Diagramação: Ponto Inicial Design Gráfico

Iconografia e tratamento de imagem: Denise Durand Kremer (ger.), Claudia Bertolazzi, Fernando Cambetas (pesquisa), Fernanda Crevin (tratamento de imagens)

Licenciamento de conteúdos de terceiros: Roberta Bento (gerente), Jenis Oh (coord.), Liliane Rodrigues e Flávia Zambon (analistas), Raísa Maris Reina (assist.)

Ilustrações: Nicolas Maia (aberturas de unidade), Ari Nicolosi, Ilustra Cartoon e Sirayama

Design: Gláucia Correa Koller (ger.), Flávia Dutra e Gustavo Vanini (proj. gráfico e capa), Erik Taketa (pós-produção)

Ilustração de capa: Estúdio Luminos

Dados Internacionais de Catalogação na Publicação (CIP)

```
Morino, Eliete Canesi
    Marcha Criança : Língua Inglesa : 1º ao 5º ano /
Eliete Canesi Morino, Rita Brugin. -- 3. ed. -- São
Paulo : Scipione, 2020.
    (Coleção Marcha Criança ; vol. 1 ao 5)

Bibliografia

1. Língua inglesa (Ensino fundamental) - Anos iniciais
I. Título II. Brugin, Rita III. Série
                                          CDD 372.652
20-1102
```

Angélica Ilacqua - Bibliotecária - CRB-8/7057

2023
Código da obra CL 745888
CAE 721149 (AL) / 721148 (PR)
ISBN 9788547403119 (AL)
ISBN 9788547403126 (PR)
3ª edição
4ª impressão
De acordo com a BNCC.

Impressão e acabamento: Bercrom Gráfica e Editora

Uma publicação

Com ilustrações de **Nicolas Maia**, seguem abaixo os créditos das fotos utilizadas nas aberturas de Unidade:

UNIDADE 1: Mochila amarela: 5 second Studio/Shutterstock, **Mochila preta:** everytime/Shutterstock, **Mochila amarela 2:** Pixel-Shot/Shutterstock, **Mochila preta 2:** Winai Tepsuttinun/Shutterstock, **Mochila vermelha:** Winai Tepsuttinun/Shutterstock, **Prancheta:** rCarner/Shutterstock, **Mochila azul-escura:** Billion Photos/Shutterstock, **Corda:** Seregam/Shutterstock, **Mochila azul-clara:** Ogovorka/Shutterstock, **Cadeira:** Aleksandr Kurganov/Shutterstock, **Mochila vermelha 2:** 3DMI/Shutterstock, **Mochila amarela 3:** Thammanoon Khamchalee/Shutterstock, **Globo terrestre:** Tanya_mtv/Shutterstock, **Lousa:** Manbetta/Shutterstock, **Corda 2:** Picsfive/Shutterstock.

UNIDADE 2: Velas de aniversário: Lunatictm/Shutterstock, **Paisagem de piquenique:** Lunatictm/Shutterstock, **Textura xadrez colorida:** sunwards/Shutterstock, **Garrafas de suco:** Nitr/Shutterstock, **Balões de festa:** artjazz/Shutterstock, **Bandeja de brigadeiros:** Bruno Martins Imagens/Shutterstock, **Estrelinhas:** s-ts/Shutterstock, **Sanduíches com pão de forma:** MaraZe/Shutterstock, **Balão de festa azul:** pukach/Shutterstock, **Bolo:** MaraZe/Shutterstock, **Bolo de aniversário:** NSC Photography/Shutterstock, **Sanduíches com baguete:** Asya Nurullina/Shutterstock.

UNIDADE 3: Fachada de prédio vermelho: Kamrad71/Shutterstock, **Cena de festa:** Roman Samborskyi/Shutterstock, **Interior de banheiro:** Witsanu S/Shutterstock, **Interior de quarto:** Photographee.eu/Shutterstock, **Interior de sala:** Yuganov Konstantin/Shutterstock, **Textura de azulejos brancos:** okawa somchai/Shutterstock, **Interior de carro:** rivermo74/Shutterstock, **Interior de escritório:** mavo/Shutterstock.

UNIDADE 4: Paisagem de parque: mikolajn/Shutterstock, **Violão:** RemarkEliza/Shutterstock, **Bicicleta:** Ivonne Wierink/Shutterstock, **Bicicleta infantil:** wk1003mike/Shutterstock, **Lixeiras para lixo reciclável:** BIRTHPIX/Shutterstock, **Garrafa plástica amassada:** Picsfive/Shutterstock, **Bola:** titelio/Shutterstock.

APRESENTAÇÃO

Querido aluno, querida aluna,

Quanto mais cedo começamos a estudar uma segunda língua, mais simples e fácil é aprendê-la.

Com a coleção **Marcha Criança – Língua Inglesa**, você descobrirá que o inglês já faz parte do dia a dia, e esperamos que você tenha prazer em aprender esse idioma, tão necessário para entender melhor o mundo em que vivemos.

Aqui você encontra um modo divertido de aprender, por meio de diversas atividades, como colagens, desenhos, pinturas, dramatizações, jogos, canções e muito mais!

Participe com entusiasmo das aulas e aproveite esta oportunidade que seu professor e esta coleção propiciam: aprender inglês de maneira bastante instigante e motivadora.

Good job!

As autoras

Nicolas Maia/Arquivo da editora

KNOW YOUR BOOK

Veja a seguir como seu livro está organizado.

UNIT

Seu livro está organizado em quatro unidades temáticas, com aberturas em páginas duplas. Cada unidade tem duas lições. As aberturas de unidade são compostas dos seguintes boxes:

JOIN THE CIRCLE!

Você e os colegas terão a oportunidade de conversar sobre a cena apresentada e a respeito do que já sabem sobre o tema da unidade.

LET'S LEARN!

Aqui você vai encontrar a lista dos conteúdos que serão estudados na unidade.

LISTEN AND SAY

Esta seção tem o propósito de fazer você observar e explorar a cena de abertura da lição. Permite também que você entre em contato com as estruturas que serão trabalhadas e desenvolva as habilidades auditiva e oral.

KEY WORDS

Este boxe apresenta nomes de objetos e de partes da cena de abertura, que serão estudados ao longo da lição.

LANGUAGE TIME

Esta seção traz atividades que vão possibilitar que você explore a língua inglesa de forma simples e natural.

NOW, WE KNOW!

Momento de verificar se os conteúdos foram compreendidos por meio de atividades diversificadas.

LET'S PRACTICE!

Esta seção propõe atividades para reforçar o que foi estudado na lição. Você vai colocar em prática o que aprendeu nas seções anteriores.

IT'S YOUR TURN!

Esta seção propõe atividades procedimentais, experiências ou vivências para você aprender na prática o conteúdo estudado.

TALKING ABOUT...

A seção traz uma seleção de temas para refletir, discutir e aprender mais, capacitando você para atuar no dia a dia com mais consciência!

REVIEW

Esta seção traz atividades de revisão de cada uma das lições.

LET'S PLAY!

Atividades lúdicas para que você aprenda enquanto se diverte!

⇉ Material complementar ⇇

READER

Livro de leitura que acompanha cada volume. A história estimula a imaginação e o conhecimento linguístico, levando você a uma aventura emocionante pelo mundo da literatura.

GLOSSARY

Traz as palavras-chave em inglês estudadas ao longo deste volume, seguidas da tradução em português.

⇉ Quando você encontrar estes ícones, fique atento! ⇇

 In pairs    In groups   Say   Stick   Write

 Draw   Circle   Make an **X**    Number   Color

 Dot to dot   Match   Listen

CONTENTS

Siriyama/Arquivo da editora

Siriyama/Arquivo da editora

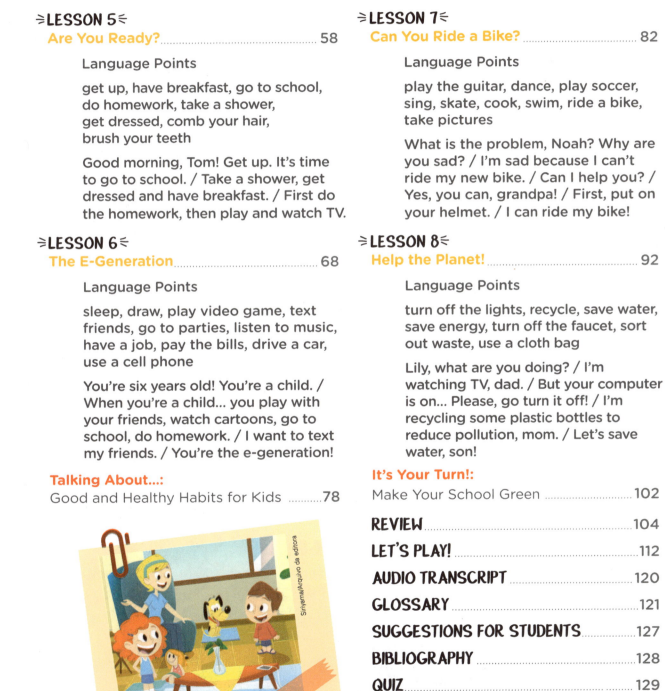

Siriyama/Arquivo da editora

SCHOOL IS COOL!

UNIT 1

Join the Circle!

- Where are they?
- Who are these people?
- What are they doing?

Let's Learn!

- School subjects
- Numbers 0 to 100
- The alphabet
- Genitive case
- School games
- There to be
- Prepositions of place
- How many...?
- Ordinal numbers 1 to 10

WHAT IS YOUR FAVORITE SUBJECT?

Listen and say

GOOD MORNING, I'M MS. JONES. I'M GLAD TO MEET YOU.

GOOD MORNING, TEACHER! WE'RE GLAD TO MEET YOU, TOO.

Math
History
Science
Lunch time
Portuguese
English
Physical Education (P.E.)

LET'S LOOK AT THIS YEAR'S CLASS SCHEDULE.

Key Words

1 Look, listen and say.

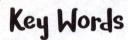

Physical Education (P.E.)

Geography

Math

English

Portuguese   History   Science   Art

Language Time

1 Listen, complete and say the numbers.

0 zero	1 one	2 two	3 three	4 four	5 five
6 six	....	8 eight	9 nine	10 ten	....
12 twelve	....	14 fourteen	....	16 sixteen	17 seventeen
18 eighteen	19 nineteen	....	....	....	50 fifty
60 sixty	....	80 eighty	90 ninety	100 one hundred	

2 Listen to the alphabet letters, point and say.

A B C D E F G H I
J K L M N O P Q R
S T U V W X Y Z

Nelson Marques/Shutterstock.

3 Talk to a classmate and act out.

HOW DO YOU SPELL "BOOK"?

B-O-O-K

Pressmaster/Shutterstock

Genitive case

This is Mary**'s** tablet.

These are Tim**'s** minicars.

4   Complete using the genitive case (**'s**). Use the clues given.

a) This is _____ bike.
(Connor)

b) This is _____ cell
phone. (my father)

c) They are _____
friends. (my sister)

d) This is _____ new
house. (my friend)

1 Read the name of the school subjects, stick and say.

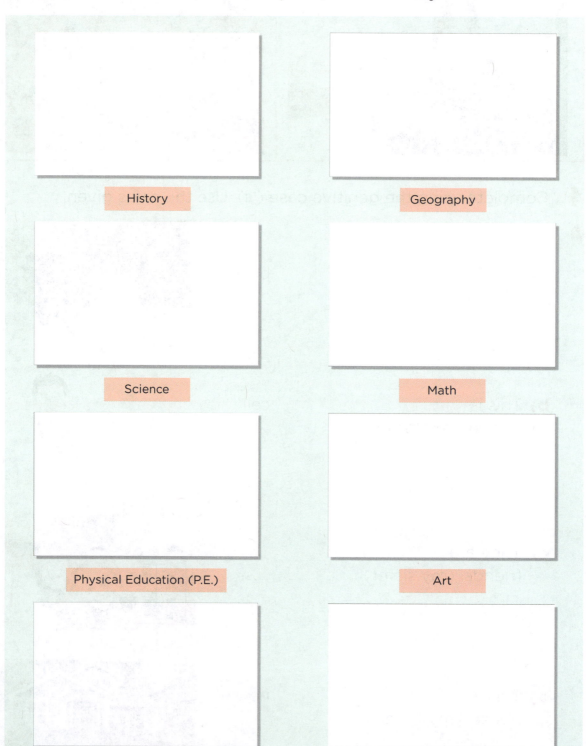

History

Geography

Science

Math

Physical Education (P.E.)

Art

Portuguese

English

2 Add and write the numbers.

a) 20 + 15 = ...

b) 25 + 75 = ...

c) 44 + 44 = ...

d) 61 + 32 = ...

3 Complete the sentences using the words from the box.

| **is Janet's dog** | **This is Lucy's** | **Steve's cat** |

Nina Buday/Shutterstock

Steve

Tuzemka/Shutterstock

Janet

HTeam/Shutterstock

Lucy

a) This is ....

b) This ....

c) .... baby brother.

4 Complete the missing letters of the words.

a) | H | I | | T | | R | |

b) | A | | |

c) | | E | O | | R | A | | H | |

d) | S | | I | | | E |

e) | E | N | | L | | S | |

f) | | | T | |

g) | | O | R | T | | G | U | | S | |

Let's Practice!

1 Write your class schedule.

Time	Mon.	Tue.	Wed.	Thu.	Fri.

My Class Schedule

Ilustra Cartoon/Arquivo da editora

2 Listen to Sophia and Emma's dialog. Then act out.

5

stockfour/Shutterstock

Sophia: What is your favorite school subject, Emma?

Emma: My favorite school subject is English, but I like Portuguese and Geography, too. And you, Sophia?

Sophia: My favorite school subjects are History and Science.

Emma: Science is cool! When is our Science class? I forgot.

Sophia: Let me see. It's on Monday at 8:00 a.m.

Emma: Thanks, Sophia.

Sophia: You're welcome!

3 In pairs, match the pictures to the sentences.

a)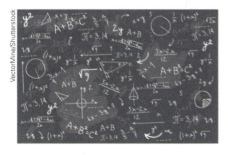

b)

c)

d)

1. My favorite school subject is English.

2. My favorite school subject is Science.

3. My favorite school subject is Geography.

4. My favorite school subject is Physical Education (P.E.).

4 Read the text quickly and circle the correct answer.

a) This kind of text is a book page / a dictionary entry.

b) This text offers information about a word / bikes.

 **bicycle** *noun*

/ˈbaɪsɪkl/

(*also informal* **bike**)

1. a road vehicle with two wheels that you ride by pushing the pedals with your feet.

Examples:

He got on his **bicycle** *and rode off.*
We went for a **bicycle ride** *on Sunday.*
She spent the day **riding her bicycle** *around the lake.* [...]

Based on: <https://www.oxfordlearnersdictionaries.com/definition/english/bicycle_1?q=bicycle> (accessed on: Feb. 12, 2020).

kvsan/Shutterstock

5 Read the text again and write **T** (true) or **F** (false).

a) There are five examples using the word bicycle in this entry. ☐

b) The informal synonym for bicycle is bike. ☐

c) You can listen to the word pronunciation. ☐

d) In a dictionary you find synonyms, word definitions and examples of sentences to help you understand the meaning of the words. ☐

e) The words are not in alphabetical order. ☐

 Tech Tips...

Watch the animation on how to use a dictionary available at: <https://www.youtube.com/watch?v=DxLh4dpARj8> (accessed on: Feb. 11, 2020).

6 In pairs, choose an English word. Then look it up in the dictionary and complete the chart below.

Word:	Definition:
....	....

| Write a sentence using the chosen word and illustrate it.

....

....

....

.... | |

Let's Sing!

The Alphabet Song!

A B C D E F G

H I J K L M N O

P Q R S T U V

W X Y Z

That's the alphabet for me.

7 Let's do a spelling bee contest!

To learn more

Spelling Bee is a famous game in which players have to spell a list of words. Kids need to memorize the spelling of words as they appear in the dictionary. This game is popular in English speaking countries.

Lorelyn Medina/Shutterstock

LESSON 2

SCHOOL GAMES

Listen and say

7

GOOD MORNING, KIDS! I AM HERE TO ANNOUNCE THE SCHOOL'S GAME WEEK!

HURRAY!!!!

KIDS, THERE ARE GAMES FOR EVERYONE!

OK, TEACHER!

OK! THE GAMES ARE HANGMAN, MUSICAL CHAIR, THREE-LEGGED RACE, EGG RACE, BINGO AND SPELLING BEE.

Key Words

1 Look, listen and say.

8

tug of war

egg race

three-legged race

musical chair

scavenger hunt

spelling bee

bingo

hangman

Language Time

1 Listen, point and say.

Ordinal numbers				
1st	2nd	3rd	4th	5th
first	second	third	fourth	fifth
6th	7th	8th	9th	10th
sixth	seventh	eighth	ninth	tenth

2 Write the ordinal numbers according to the picture.

AMj Studio/Arquivo da editora

a) Grace is the .... student in class.

b) Mary is the .... student in class.

c) Sue is the .... student in class.

d) Conrad is the .... student in class.

e) Todd is the .... student in class.

f) Chris is the .... student in class.

There to be		
Affirmative	Negative	Interrogative
There is	There is not (There isn't)	Is there...?
There are	There are not (There aren't)	Are there...?

3 How many books are there in the bookshelf? Complete with *there to be*.

Ilustra Cartoon/Arquivo da editora

a) .... Portuguese book.

b) .... Math books.

c) .... English books.

4 Read the prepositions of place chart. Then read and draw.

behind	between	in	on	under

a) a ball in a box	**b)** a pencil on a desk	**c)** a boy behind a table	**d)** a schoolbag under a chair	**e)** an eraser between two pens

Now, We Know!

1 Write the abbreviations of the ordinal numbers.

a) fifth ....

b) eighth ....

c) ninth ....

d) second ....

e) third ....

f) first ....

g) tenth ....

h) fourth ....

2 Complete the sentences with the ordinal numbers from activity 1 in full.

Pretty Vectors/Shutterstock

a) Saturday is the .... day of the week.

b) Monday is the .... day of the week.

c) Thursday is the .... day of the week.

d) Tuesday is the .... day of the week.

e) Sunday is the .... day of the week.

f) Friday is the .... day of the week.

g) Wednesday is the .... day of the week.

3 Look at the picture and answer the questions.

a) Where is the History book?

....

b) Where is the Art book?

....

c) Where is the mouse?

....

d) Where is the mouse pad?

....

e) Where is the computer?

....

f) Where are your books?

....

Let's Practice!

1 Read the sentences and circle the correct picture.

a) The clock is behind the boy.

b) The boy's schoolbag is under his desk.

c) The notebooks are in the schoolbag.

d) The girl is behind the curtain.

e) The teacher is standing between two students in the classroom.

2 Unscramble the name of the games and write.

a) gut of raw

b) gge cera

c) hteer ggleed ecar

d) clamsiu hcira

e) ngllsepi eeb

f) anhgnam

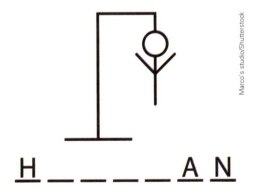

H _ _ _ _ A N

3 Use the glossary and match the pictures to the words.

a) throw a pebble   **b)** rocks   **c)** pieces of chalk

nito/Shutterstock

Sonya illustration/Shutterstock

MsDianaZ/Shutterstock

4 Read the text and make an **X**.

Teguh Mujiono/Shutterstock

Hopscotch's rules

1. First use the chalk to draw the hopscotch grid on the ground.

2. Next write the numbers from 1 to 10 on the grid and the word STOP.

3. Throw a small pebble (beanbag, small object) to land inside a square and jump in one or two legs – depending on where the pebble falls – to get there.

4. If the pebble touches the border of the grid, you miss your turn. Give the pebble to the next player.

5. Jump through the squares skipping the one with the pebble.

6. Pick up the pebble on your way back. The first player to reach STOP is the winner.

a) To play hopscotch you need ....

☐ a pebble   ☐ a pebble and a piece of chalk

b) You need to .... to play hopscotch.

☐ dance   ☐ jump

c) You win hopscotch when you are in the ....

☐ Stop square   ☐ second square

5 Draw your favorite game and complete.

My favorite game is ....

To play this game you need ....

....

 Let's Sing!

Playing with Friends

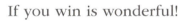

I love to play with all my friends,

I never, never play alone,

Because... I have many friends,

I never, never play alone.

When you play a game,

Don't mind which game,

Sometimes you lose,

Sometimes you win.

If you win is wonderful!

If you lose, don't be sad!

Respect your friends

And always have fun!

Respect your friends

And always have fun!

Arak Rattanawijittakorn/Shutterstock

Play Fair!

- What do these pictures represent?

- Do you think fair play attitudes are important? Why?
- Do you play fair? Share some examples with your classmates.

1 Read the list below and make and **X** in the alternatives that demonstrate fair play.

a) respect ☐

b) cheating ☐

c) violence ☐

d) obey the rules ☐

e) integrity ☐

f) solidarity ☐

g) bad behavior ☐

h) tolerance ☐

i) equality ☐

j) jealousy ☐

2 Make a word cloud pannel with fair play words.

Banco de imagens/Arquivo da editora

UNIT 2

SOCIAL LIFE

Join the Circle!

- Where are they?
- Who are these people?
- What are they doing?

Let's Learn!

- Birthday party items
- Days of the week
- Months and dates
- Ordinal numbers 1 to 30
- Picnic food
- Seasons of the year
- *Wh-* questions
- Demonstrative pronouns
- Verb to be (interrogative)
- Verb have (affirmative)

LESSON 3

A BIRTHDAY PARTY

Listen and say

Key Words

1 Look, listen and say.

| sandwiches | sweets | cake | balloons | guests |

sing "Happy Birthday" blow out candles open gifts dance and play games

Language Time

1 Listen and say the ordinal numbers.

1st first	2nd second	3rd third	4th fourth	5th fifth
6th sixth	7th seventh	8th eighth	9th ninth	10th tenth
11th eleventh	12th twelfth	13th thirteenth	14th fourteenth	15th fifteenth
16th sixteenth	17th seventeenth	18th eighteenth	19th nineteenth	20th twentieth
21st twenty-first	22nd twenty-second	23rd twenty-third	24th twenty-fourth	30th thirtieth

2 Listen and say the months of the year and the days of the week.

Months of the year					
January	February	March	April	May	June
July	August	September	October	November	December

Days of the week						
Sunday	Monday	Tuesday	Wednesday	Thursday	Friday	Saturday

3 Read and say the dates.

The first day of January
January 1st (January the first)

The second day of April
April 2nd (April the second)

The third day of March
March 3rd (March the third)

The fourth day of February
February 4th
(February the fourth)

4 Match the dates.

a) The first day of May

b) The tenth day of April

c) The fifth day of March

d) The thirty-first day of December

	December 31st
	May 1st
	April 10th
	March 5th

Verb to be – Interrogative form	Short answers
Is your birthday in May, Mike?	Yes, it is.
Is today Friday?	No, it isn't
Are you at school now?	Yes, I am.
Are Martha and Carla your sisters?	No, they aren't.

5 Look at the pictures and answer using short answers.

a) Is it a birthday hat?

Tribalium/Shutterstock

b) Are they balloons?

Beautyimage/Shutterstock

c) Is today March 11th?

iCreative3D/Shutterstock

d) Is today Tuesday?

Alexander Lysenko/Shutterstock

Now, We Know!

1 Complete the crossword with the months of the year.

Across and down numbered cells: 10th, 5th, 3rd, 6th, 11th, 8th, 2nd, 4th, 1st, 9th, 12th, 7th

2 Look at the Brazilian calendar and complete the sentences.

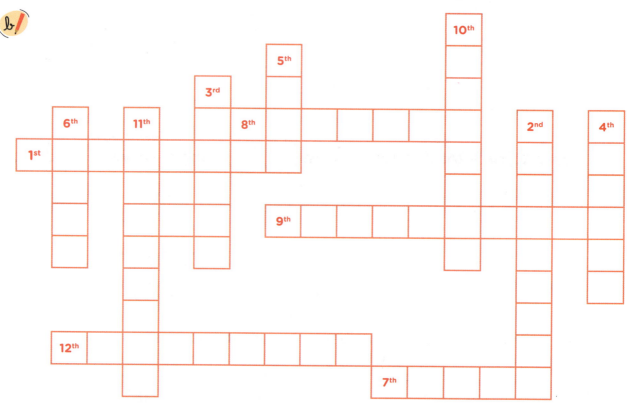

January	February	March	April	May	June
Maksym Yukhymets/ Shutterstock	Maksym Yukhymets/ Shutterstock	Ocelot/Shutterstock	Ocelot/Shutterstock	MatoomMi/ Shutterstock	Ilustra Cartoon/ Arquivo da editora
July	August	September	October	November	December
Ilustra Cartoon/ Arquivo da editora	Ilustra Cartoon/ Arquivo da editora	MicroOne/ Shutterstock	MicroOne/ Shutterstock	MicroOne/ Shutterstock	Iconic Bestiary/ Shutterstock

a) Christmas is in ....

b) Mother's Day is in ....

c) Spring is in ....

d) Winter is in ....

3 Write the dates in full. What date is it?

a)

....

b)

....

c)

....

d)

....

e)

....

f)

....

4 Talk to three classmates and complete the birthday chart.

When is your birthday?

It's in ....

Classmates' names:			
Classmates' birthday dates:			

Let's Practice!

1 Let's play bingo!

April 5th	March 22nd	October 15th	November 11th	December 23rd
June 9th	August 6th	January 31st	May 12th	September 20th
February 18th	July 19th	October 8th	December 25th	August 27th

Bingo chart

2 Listen and act out.

Alexa: When is your birthday, Adrian?

Adrian: It's next Saturday, June 12th.

Alexa: What time is your party?

Adrian: It's at 7:00 p.m.

Alexa: Where is the party?

Adrian: It's at my house.

Alexa: See on Saturday, Adrian.

Adrian: See you, Alexa. Bye.

Alexa: Bye.

3 What kind of information can you find in an invitation card? Read and make an **X**.

a) The address of the school. ☐

b) The days of the week and time. ☐

c) The date, address, time, day of the week of the event and the person's name. ☐

4 Read the text and answer.

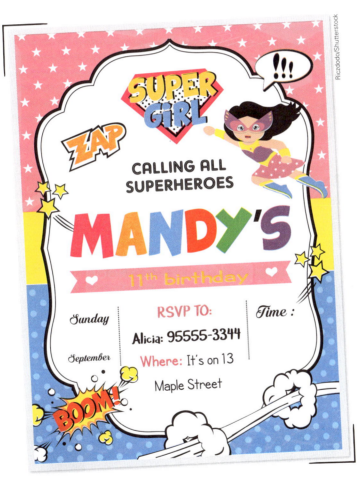

Riczdodo/Shutterstock

a) What is the invitation for? ....

b) When is the party? ....

c) What time is the party? ....

d) Where is the party? ....

5 Create a birthday invitation card.

To learn more

People all over the world celebrate birthdays, but they do it in different ways.

In Mexico, most birthday boys and girls break a party *piñata*, which is full of sweets. In Senegal, the party has a lot of meat. In Sweden, they have cakes and candles in the morning, and in China they eat birthday noodles to have a long happy life.

6 Look at the pictures and write the name of the country.

a)

wavebreakmedia/Shutterstock

b)

Anna_Pustynnikova/Shutterstock

Let's Sing!

Your Birthday Song!

It's your birthday today.

It's your birthday today.

It's your birthday today.

Happy birthday, Carol!

One, two, three, four,

Five, six, seven, eight,

Nine years old!

Now you're nine years old!

Happy birthday, Carol!

Ilustrações: Ari Nicolosi/Arquivo da editora

7 Read and circle **YES** or **NO**.

a) Carol's birthday is today.　　　Yes　No

b) Carol is 8 years old.　　　Yes　No

c) There are four guests in Carol's party.　　　Yes　No

d) There are no balloons and party hats in the picture.　　　Yes　No

THE PICNIC

Listen and say

BOYS AND GIRLS... LET'S HAVE A CLASS IN THE PARK TODAY.

HURRAY!!!!

IT'S SPRING... WE CAN SEE DIFFERENT SPECIES OF FLOWERS, BIRDS AND INSECTS IN THIS SEASON.

Key Words

1 Look, listen and say.

orange juice

cookies

carrot cake

tuna sandwich

spinach pie   chicken wrap   watermelon   grapes

Language Time

1 Stick and say the name of the seasons of the year.

Seasons of the year

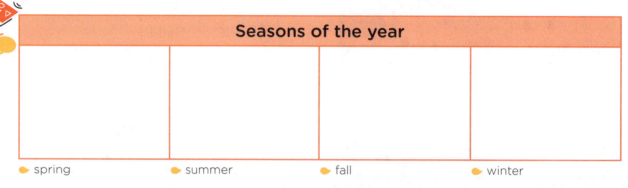

● spring   ● summer   ● fall   ● winter

Demonstrative pronouns

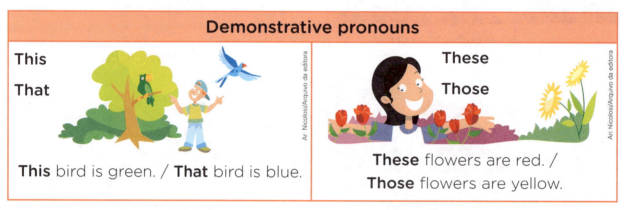

This
That

This bird is green. / **That** bird is blue.

These
Those

These flowers are red. /
Those flowers are yellow.

2 Complete with the pronouns *this*, *these*, *that* or *those*.

a) .... ant is red.

b) .... ants are black.

c) .... red ant is big.

d) .... ants are hungry.

Oh, no... My cake!

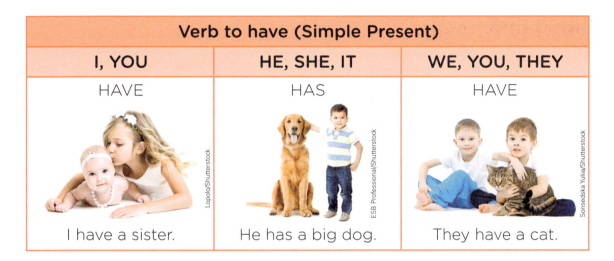

Verb to have (Simple Present)		
I, YOU	**HE, SHE, IT**	**WE, YOU, THEY**
HAVE	HAS	HAVE
I have a sister.	He has a big dog.	They have a cat.

3 Complete the sentences using the verb form *have* or *has*.

a)

The boy _____ a bike.

b)

They _____ a big house.

c)

I _____ three balloons.

d)

He _____ a car.

Now, We Know!

1 Unscramble the words and write the seasons. Then match to the pictures.

a) mermsu ....

b) ingrsp ....

c) terinw ....

d) lalf ....

MicroOne/Shutterstock

Melody A/Shutterstock

ecco/Shutterstock

Naumova Marina/Shutterstock

2 Read and make an **X**.

a) In this season, there are lots of beautiful flowers.

☐ spring   ☐ winter   ☐ fall   ☐ summer

b) The sun is very hot in this season.

☐ spring   ☐ winter   ☐ fall   ☐ summer

c) This is the season of tree leaves falling.

☐ spring   ☐ winter   ☐ fall   ☐ summer

d) It's very cold in this season.

☐ spring   ☐ winter   ☐ fall   ☐ summer

e) My favorite season of the year is ....

☐ spring   ☐ winter   ☐ fall   ☐ summer

3 Put the sentences in order.

a) brothers / three / she / has / .

....

b) have / I / sister / a / beautiful / .

....

c) a / new / game / Jim / has / board / .

....

d) car / they / a / big / have / .

....

4 Look and write *this*, *these*, *that* or *those*.

a) .... are healthy fruits to eat.

b) .... is a delicious red apple.

c) .... are juicy peaches.

d) .... are green and red grapes.

Let's Practice!

1 Read and put the dialog in order. Then listen to correct it.

( ) Hello, Sebastian. I'm fine, thanks. And you?

( ) What is your favorite season of the year?

( ) Why?

( ) Yes, I would love to go to the beach.

( ) Hi, Julia! How are you?

( ) Because I like the beach. Would you like to go to the beach with me and my family next weekend?

( ) It is summer.

( ) I'm fine, thanks.

Lisa F. Young/Shutterstock

2 Complete with the correct form of the verb *have*.

a) Mary .... six colored pencils.

b) Grandpa .... a blue bird pet.

c) Mark and Cecilia .... new schoolbags.

d) We .... breakfast at 7 o'clock.

e) I .... three new toy cars.

f) My dog .... a long tail.

3 Listen to Bob and his mom planning a picnic. Circle the items they need to buy.

Markus Mainka/Shutterstock

AlfazetChronicles/Shutterstock

Anna Kucherova/Shutterstock

Neonic Flower/Shutterstock

Nattika/Shutterstock

andersphoto/Shutterstock

4 In groups, it's time to plan your picnic.

Our picnic: ....

Place: ....

Date: ....

People: ....

Alexander Raths/Shutterstock

....

Picnic items list: ....

....

5 Read and match.

a) cut   **b)** peel   **c)** put together

☐   ☐   ☐

6 Read the text.

FRUIT SALAD ON A STICK

Prep. Time: **15 min**

Ingredients

5 bananas, 5 apples, 5 oranges,
20 green grapes, 10 strawberries,
4 kiwis
20 barbecue wooden sticks

How to prepare

- Peel the bananas, the apples, the oranges and the kiwis. Cut them in cubes and reserve.

- Wash the grapes and the strawberries. Slice the strawberries in half. Then put the fruit pieces on barbecue sticks.

7 Read and circle the correct answer.

a) The fruit salad on a stick is *very healthy* / *not healthy*.

b) To prepare it you need *cheese* / *fruits you like*.

c) To make the fruit salad you need to *cut the fruits* / *peel the vegetables*.

8 Draw your favorite food and the ingredients you need to prepare it.

 Let's Sing!

Fun and Picnic

You have fun, you have fun

When you plan a picnic.

Apples, chips, cookies,

Pop sodas and sandwiches.

You have fun, you have fun

When you go to a picnic.

You sing a lot, play and eat

With your friends in a picnic.

wavebreakmedia/Shutterstock

Let's Make a Birthday Scrapbook!

 Follow the steps below to create a birthday scrapbook.

Katrina Brown/Shutterstock

YOU NEED:

- White cardboard cut in a square (30 cm × 30 cm)

Tokarchuk Andrii/Shutterstock

- Scraps of colored papers

AVS-Images/Shutterstock

- Colored markers

Kucher Serhii/Shutterstock

- Glue

Mega Pixel/Shutterstock

- Scissors

Kozak Sergii/Shutterstock

- Colored pencils

Peter Hermes Furian/Shutterstock

- Personal birthday photos

Photographee.eu/Shutterstock

1) Cut the white cardboard in 30 cm x 30 cm shape.

2) Glue the birthday photos.

3) Decorate the scrapbook using colored pencils and markers.

4) Use the scraps of colored paper to decorate it.

5) Write captions describing the photos and write under them.

Ilustrações: Ilustra Cartoon/Arquivo da editora

GROWING UP

Join the Circle!
- Where are they?
- Who are these people?
- What are they doing?

Let's Learn!
- Daily routines
- Imperatives
- Telling the time
- Verb to be (all forms)

ARE YOU READY?

Listen and say

Key Words

1 Look, listen and say.

get up

have breakfast

go to school

do homework

take a shower

get dressed

comb your hair

brush your teeth

Language Time

Imperatives

Get up, Tim!

Take a quick shower.

Eat your lunch and drink your juice.

Do your Science homework.

Ilustrações: yatate/Shutterstock

1 Write imperative sentences using the ones from the box.

> **Get up, please.**   **Play the game.**
> **Do your homework.**   **Brush your teeth.**

a)

didesign021/Shutterstock

....

b)

carballo/Shutterstock

....

c)

sirikorn thamniyom/Shutterstock

d)

Monkey Business Images/Shutterstock

2 Listen and say the time. What time is it?

5:00	It's five o'clock.	**5:30**	It's five thirty.
5:05	It's five five.	**5:35**	It's five thirty-five.
5:10	It's five ten.	**5:40**	It's five forty.
5:15	It's five fifteen.	**5:45**	It's five forty-five.
5:20	It's five twenty.	**5:50**	It's five fifty.
5:25	It's five twenty-five.	**5:55**	It's five fifty-five.

midday (a.m.)	**midnight (p.m.)**
It's midday. It's time for lunch!	It's midnight. Have good dreams!

bulatova/Shutterstock

3 What time is it? Write the time in full.

a)

It's two forty-five.

b)

....

c)

....

d)

....

Ilustrações: Ilustra Cartoon/Arquivo da editora

Now, We Know!

1 Look at the pictures, listen and make an **X**.

a)
   □      □

b)
   □      □

c)
   □   □

d)
   □      □

Ilustrações: Cartoon/Arquivo da editora

2 Listen to the dialog and act out.

Philip: What time do you get up, Lucy?

Lucy: I get up at 5.30 a.m., then I take a shower, brush my teeth, have breakfast, get dressed and go to school.

Philip: 5:30 a.m.? That is too early!

Lucy: Yes, it is. And you? What time do you usually get up?

Philip: Well, I get up at six o'clock, then I take a shower, brush my teeth, have breakfast, get dressed and I walk to school with my brothers.

Syda Productions/Shutterstock

3 Look at the clocks and write the time.

a)

....

b)

....

c)

....

d)

....

4 What time is it now?

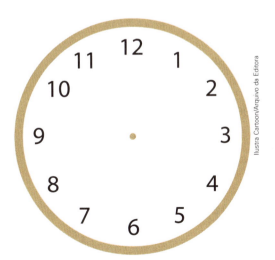

It's ....

Let's Practice!

1 Draw the clock hands and complete the sentences. My daily routine.

a) I get up at ....

b) I take a shower at ....

c) I have breakfast at ....

d) I go to school at ....

e) I have lunch at ....

f) I do my homework at ....

g) I play at ....

h) I watch TV at ....

i) I have dinner at ....

j) I go to bed at ....

Ilustrações: AMj Studio/Arquivo da editora

2 Write your routines and share with a classmate.

a) Three morning routines: ....

b) Two evening routines: ....

3 Read about Lianne's daily routine.

My name is Lianne. I'm 10 years old. This is my new daily routine. I am in a new school this year and I have a busy day. I get up at 6:30 a.m. every day. Then I take a shower, brush my teeth, get dressed and have a big breakfast with fruit, milk and sandwiches. After that, I brush my teeth again. It's important to brush your teeth after every meal! Then I comb my hair and walk to school. My classes start at 8:00 a.m.

I have lunch at school and come back home at 3.30 p.m. After that, I do my homework, I play with my dog, I have dinner with my family and go to sleep at 10:00 p.m. What a busy day!

sutlafk/Shutterstock

4 Number the items according to Lianne's morning routine.

a) have breakfast ☐   **b)** brush the teeth again ☐

c) get dressed ☐   **d)** get up ☐

e) take a shower ☐   **f)** walk to school ☐

g) brush the teeth ☐   **h)** comb the hair ☐

The Mulberry Bush

27 Here we go round the mulberry bush,

The mulberry bush, the mulberry bush.

Here we go round the mulberry bush

So early in the morning.

This is the way we take a shower,

We take a shower, we take a shower.

This is the way we take a shower

Every Sunday morning.

This is the way we walk to school,

We walk to school, we walk to school.

This is the way we walk to school

Every Monday morning.

This is the way we drink our milk,

We drink our milk, we drink our milk.

This is the way we drink our milk

Every Tuesday morning.

This is the way we read our books,

We read our books, we read our books.

This is the way we read our books

Every Wednesday morning.

This is the way we eat some bread,

We eat some bread, we eat some bread.

This is the way we eat some bread

Every Thursday morning.

This is the way we write our names

We write our names, we write our names.

This is the way we write our names

Every Friday morning.

This is the way we have our lunch,

We have our lunch, we have our lunch.

This is the way we have our lunch

Every Saturday morning.

 LESSON **6**

THE E-GENERATION

Listen and say

28

Key Words

1 Look, listen and say.

29

| sleep | draw | play video game | text friends | go to parties |

| listen to music | have a job | pay the bills | drive a car | use a cell phone |

Language Time

Verb to be						
Affirmative	I am	You are	He/She/It is	We are	You are	They are
Negative	I am not I'm not	You are not You aren't	He/She/It is not / isn't	We are not We aren't	You are not You aren't	They are not They aren't
Interrogative	Am I?	Are you?	Is he/she/it?	Are we?	Are you?	Are they?
Examples	**He is** my friend. **Is he** my friend? **He is not** (**isn't**) my friend. **They are** in the classroom. **Are they** in the classroom? **They are not** (**aren't**) in the classroom.					

1 Complete the sentences using *am*, *is*, *are*, *isn't* or *aren't*.

a) They .... my dogs.

b) It .... very hot.

c) I .... very happy.

d) We .... best friends.

e) She .... at school.

2 Circle the correct form of the verb *to be*.

a) I *am / are* an engineer.

b) Susan *are / isn't* our English teacher. (not)

c) Peter and Grace *are / aren't* Canadians. (not)

d) My favorite kind of food *isn't / is* pizza. (not)

e) I *am not / am* French. I *am not / am* from Brazil. (not)

f) Mary and Taylor *are / aren't* cousins.

3 Complete the text with the correct form of the verb *to be*.

We .... best friends. We .... at home. We .... at school. Our names .... Mike, Jenny and Steve.

Mike .... in our class, but he .... our friend.

He .... good at Math, but he .... good at sports.

He .... the best soccer player in our school.

Jenny .... good at Math and she loves computer games.

Steve .... good at acting. He wants to be an actor.

Now, We Know!

1 Listen and number the pictures.

a)

b)

c)

d)

e)

f)

g)

h)

2 Read and order the sentences. Then write them.

a) you / a / teenager / are / ?

....

b) Tom / child / is / a / .

....

c) friends / grown-ups / my / aren't / .

....

d) Ms. Jones / a / teacher / is / .

....

e) in the / are / the / kids / classroom / .

....

f) is / best / Bart / friend / my / .

....

3 Play the *Guessing game* with your classmates. Follow your teacher's orientation.

Lorelyn Medina/Shutterstock

Let's Practice!

1 Read, listen and act out.

2 Fill in the blanks with *am*, *is* or *are*.

Dear Ms. Jones,

I .... Janet Lee. Oliver, Lara and Paul Lee .... my

children.

Oliver and Lara are at school at the moment, but Paul ....

at home with me. He .... not feeling well today. He ....

in bed resting now. He has a fever. Please send me his homework.

Thank you!

Yours sincerely,
Janet Lee

3 Answer the questions. Share your answers with a classmate.

a) Do you like to read comic strips? Which ones?

b) Who is your favorite comic strip character?

c) Where can you find comic strips?

4 Read the text and then make an **X**.

a) Jon and Garfield love routine.

☐ Yes   ☐ No

b) Jon is happy this morning.

☐ Yess   ☐ No

To learn more

Garfield is a creation of the cartoonist Jim Davis. Garfield is a fat, lazy, orange cat that loves lasagna. Jim Davis says that Garfield is a little bit of all the cats he remembered from his childhood.

5 Now create your own comic strip.

Let's Sing!

That's Life

That's Life
A baby, a child, a teenager
Or a grown-up?
Babies cry, sleep and play.
Children play, watch TV,
Do the homework.
Teenagers date, chat on the net,
And go to the disco.
Grown-ups work
Have jobs,
Drive cars,
And pay lots of bills.

Ilustrações: Cartoon/Arquivo da editora

Good and Healthy Habits for Kids

- What do these pictures represent?
- Do you make healthy choices in your life?
- Do you have attitudes that promote good family life? Explain.

1 Check the good habits of healthy kids.

(×/)

a) Go to sleep and wake up late. ☐

Go to sleep and wake up early. ☐

b) Prepare meals and eat at the right times. ☐

Skip meals during the day. ☐

c) Eat a variety of nutritional food. ☐

Eat unhealthy, low nutritional value food. ☐

d) Spend the day watching TV. ☐

Enjoy fresh air and exercise. ☐

e) Have a respectful and loving family life. ☐

Do not respect the elders in your family. ☐

f) Spend many hours playing computer games. ☐

Spend less than 2 hours a day playing video and computer games. ☐

g) Do regular, fun things together as a family and share a laugh! ☐

Don't do regular fun things together as a family. ☐

THINK GREEN

Join the Circle!
- Where are they?
- Who are these people?
- What are they doing?

Let's Learn!
- Greetings
- Hobbies
- Can (ability – all forms)
- Daily and sustainable actions
- Opposite adjectives
- Feelings
- Present Continuous (all forms)

CAN YOU RIDE A BIKE?

Listen and say

GOOD MORNING, GRANDPA.

GOOD MORNING, NOAH.

WHAT IS THE PROBLEM? WHY ARE YOU SAD?

I'M SAD BECAUSE I CAN'T RIDE MY NEW BIKE.

CAN I HELP YOU?

YES, YOU CAN, GRANDPA!

FIRST, PUT ON YOUR HELMET.

YES, GRANDPA!

Key Words

1 Look, listen and say.

play the guitar

dance

play soccer

sing

Brian A Jackson/Shutterstock

Africa Studio/Shutterstock

Fotokostic/Shutterstock

Pixel-Shot/Shutterstock

| skate | cook | swim | ride a bike | take pictures |

Language Time

1 Read the chart.

Can (Simple present)	
Affirmative	 They can dance ballet.
Negative	 He can't ride a bike.
Interrogative	 Can he sing?
Short forms	Yes, I can. / No, I can't.

2 Look at the pictures and complete the sentences with *can* or *can't*.

a) They .... swim.

b) Johnny .... play soccer.

c) Lucy .... drive a car.

3 Look at the pictures and match the opposites.

fat

small

tall

thin

big

ugly

new

short

beautiful

old

Now, We Know!

1 Look at the pictures and complete the sentences using the words from the box.

can skate	can ride their bikes	can't sing
can't bake cookies	can dance well	

a) Mary ....

....

b) Paul and Janine ....

....

c) Carla ....

....

d) The kids ....

....

e) Kathy and Gina ....

....

f) I can .... and I can't ....

2 Circle the correct adjectives to complete the sentences.

a) My bike is *new* / *ugly* / *old*.

b) My house is *small* / *tall* / *big*.

c) My cat is *ugly* / *fat* / *short*.

d) My brother is *tall* / *small* / *thin*.

e) The sneakers are *old* / *new* / *tall*.

Let's Practice!

1 Listen to some people say what they *can* and *can't* do. Then check.

chekart/Shutterstock

	Katie	Jeff	Susan	John	Alan
Can					
Can't					

2 Interview four classmates. Ask what they *can* and *can't* do.

Classmates' names	ann131313/Shutterstock	tynyuk/Shutterstock	yusufdemirci/Shutterstock	Lyudmyla Kharlamova/Shutterstock

3 Fill in the gaps using the words from the box.

	small	new	thin	pretty	
tall	big	old	short	fat	ugly

I'M ....

TED IS ....

I'M ....

MY COUSIN IS

....

MY SANDWICH IS

....

MY SANDWICH IS

....

MY CAR IS

....

MY CAR IS

....

THE PRINCESS IS

....

THE WITCH IS

....

Ilustrações: AMJ Studio/Arquivo da editora

4 Answer the questions. Then share them with a classmate.

a) Do you have a bike?

b) How often and where do you ride your bike?

5 Read the text.

www.marchacrianca.com/riding a bike

Riding a bike is a great way to connect with nature and feel good. If you ride a bike to school or work, you can save the environment by not generating any pollution. Bikes are really the best!

Bikes are the best way to save energy and make you feel good. They are a good type of transportation because you don't need to use gasoline. They are pretty, fun and provide healthy exercising. They are good for your mind and body. So, ride your bike in the park, at the beach or in the countryside. You can have a great time with your family, too!

You can exercise, have fun and save the planet! Make sure you have your helmet on, in case you fall.

6 Read the sentences and check **Yes** or **No**.

a) Bikes aren't friends of nature.

Yes ☐   No ☐

b) Bikes don't need gasoline.

Yes ☐   No ☐

c) Bikes can't help save the planet.

Yes ☐   No ☐

d) Bikes are healthy choices because you can exercise and have fun.

Yes ☐   No ☐

7 Draw your bike or your dream bike.

Feelings

I'm angry.
Oh! Oh! I'm not.
I'm happy,
happy a lot.

I'm sad.
No! No! I'm not.
I'm tired.
Yes, a lot.

I'm naughty.
Naughty, very naughty.
Yes, everyone says: "a lot".

Ilustrações: AMJ Studio/Arquivo da editora

HELP THE PLANET!

Listen and say

37

LILY, WHAT ARE YOU DOING?

I'M WATCHING TV, DAD.

BUT YOUR COMPUTER IS ON...
PLEASE, GO TURN IT OFF!

SORRY, DAD,
I'M GOING!

WHERE IS
NOAH, ANNIE?

HE'S IN THE BATHROOM,
STEVE. HE'S BRUSHING
HIS TEETH.

Key Words

1 Look, listen and say.

38

turn off the lights

recycle

save water

save energy

turn off the faucet

sort out waste

use a cloth bag

Language Time

1 Read the chart with the *Present Continuous* form.

Affirmative	Interrogative	Negative	Short answers
I am dancing.	Are you dancing?	I'm not (am not) dancing.	Yes, I am. No, I'm not.
He is studying Math.	Is he studying Math?	He isn't (is not) studying.	Yes, he is. No, he isn't.
They are singing.	Are they singing?	They aren't (are not) singing.	Yes, they are. No, they aren't.

2 Find 5 verbs in the *-ing* form and complete the sentences.

H	W	C	O	O	K	I	N	G
A	D	F	J	L	Z	X	Y	O
V	S	W	I	M	M	I	N	G
I	H	D	E	O	U	P	Y	A
N	W	A	T	C	H	I	N	G
G	T	D	O	I	N	G	B	M

a) Peter is .... cartoons on TV.

b) I am .... breakfast.

c) Rose is .... her homework.

d) Charlie and Kim are .... dinner now.

e) They are .... at the sports club.

3 Write the sentences according to the pictures.

> **She's saving water.   They're recycling.   He's turning off the lights.**

a)

....

b)

....

c)

....

4 Listen and stick the pictures.

a)

b)

c)

d)

Now, We Know!

1 Look at the picture, read and write **True** or **False**.

Today is Saturday.

My sister Mary is listening to music in her bedroom and my brother Johnny is playing with his friends outside.

I am texting my friends.

Mom is cooking lunch and Dad is cleaning the garage.

My grandpa and grandma are sleeping in the living room.

And the TV is turned on... Oh, gosh!

a) Mary and Johnny are playing in the bedroom. ....

b) Mom and dad are in the kitchen. ....

c) Dad is cleaning the garage. ....

d) Grandpa and grandma are sleeping. ....

e) The TV is turned off. ....

f) Today is Sunday. ....

2 Write the questions and complete the answers.

a) .... They are ....

b) .... She is ....

c) .... The children are ....

d) .... Matt is .... his homework.

e) .... I am .... off the lights.

Let's Practice!

1 Read, listen and act out.

Millie: Hello!

Tom: Hello!

Millie: Is that you, Tom?

Tom: Yes, it's me, Millie.

Millie: Where is Lily?

Tom: Lily is in the kitchen.

Millie: What is she doing?

Tom: She's hungry. She's making a sandwich.

Millie: And you, what are you doing?

Tom: I am playing video game.

Millie: Oh, sorry…

Now ask your classmates. What are you doing?

2 Play the *Guessing game*.

3 Complete the sentences using the *Present Continuous* of the verbs from the box. Then match the pictures.

eat	do	clean	play	help	turn off

a) Tom .... his bedroom now.

b) Harry .... soccer at the moment.

c) The kids .... a healthy lunch.

d) Molly .... her mom in the kitchen.

e) Steve .... his English homework now.

f) Patrick .... the yard faucet.

4 Read the text quickly and choose the best slogan for it.

a) Turn on the lights. ☐

b) Don't sort out the trash. ☐

c) Reduce, Reuse, Recycle! ☐

5 Read the text and answer *yes* or *no*.

100%
BIO
PRODUCT

100% CERTIFIED ECO PRODUCT
HEALTHY FOOD ONLY

THE GREEN SCHOOL TEAM!

Is your school green? We can help you!

We are the green school team. We help students and teachers make schools environment-friendly. We can help you to implement the 3 sustainability "Rs" and to save energy and water. We aim at sustainable actions!

Come and join our meetings. Be part of our team!

Meetings are every day at 11:00 a.m.

FREE on Sundays at 10:30 a.m.

Find out more at www.marchacrianca.greenteam.org.br

Don't wait anymore!

We can visit your school! Join us and let's save the planet!

a) The green team is a soccer team. ....

b) The green team can help your school to be green. ....

c) The green team workshops are free only on Sundays. ....

d) The workshops are in the afternoon. ....

6 Complete the sentence.

The 3 "Rs" are: ....

Let's Sing!

Save the Planet!

(41)

If you turn off the lights,
You save energy, energy.
If you switch off the tap,
You save water, water.

If you see a piece of litter,
Pick it up, pick it up.
(And) you will make the planet
Be better, be better.

7 Put the words in order. Then write full sentences.

a)

is   Lily   faucet   off   turning   the

....

b)

they   recycling   their   are   garbage

....

c)

lights   turning   is   the   on   Tom

....

IT'S YOUR TURN!

Make Your School Green

 Follow the steps below.

YOU NEED:

- A piece of white cardboard (30 cm x 20 cm)

Ridkous Mykhail/Shutterstock

- Scissors

StudioByTheSea/Shutterstock

- Markers

NoraphatPhotoss/Shutterstock

- Colored pencils

picoStudio/Shutterstock

1) Cut the white cardboard in 30 cm x 20 cm shape.

2) Write down the slogan and suggestions about preserving the environment.

3) Decorate the flyer using colored pencils and markers. You can make a decorative frame if you want.

4) Show your flyer to your classmates.

1 Look at the pictures and write the name of the school subject.

a)

b)

c)

d)

e)

f)

2 Check the correct answer.

a) This is _____ new red T-shirt. ☐ Daniel's ☐ Daniel

b) My _____ old car is beautiful. ☐ grandpa ☐ grandpa's

c) _____ eyes are light blue. ☐ Cathy's ☐ Cathy

d) _____ new house is big. ☐ Carl ☐ Carl's

REVIEW → School Games

1 Unscramble the words and write the name of the games.

a) ognib ....

b) geg cera ....

c) manhgan ....

d) lingleps ebe ....

e) gerscaven tunh ....

f) calsimu riach ....

g) gut fo awr ....

2 Complete the gaps with *there is* or *there are*.

a) .... one English dictionary in the bookshelf.

b) .... two Geography Atlas in the classroom.

c) .... five notebooks inside my schoolbag.

d) .... one green eraser on my desk.

e) .... thirty-five students in my class.

3 Circle the correct ordinal numbers.

a) 1st –   fifth   first   tenth

b) 3rd –   third   fourth   sixth

c) 9th –   seventh   second   ninth

d) 8th –   eighth   fifth   sixth

REVIEW ⤳ A Birthday Party

1 Match the sentence parts.

a) How ☐ are you? I'm at school.

b) Where ☐ are you? I'm fine, thanks.

c) How many ☐ are you? I'm ten years old.

d) How old ☐ students are there in your classroom? There are twenty-five.

e) When ☐ is it? It's 7:00 p.m.

f) What time ☐ is your birthday? It's on August 10th.

2 Answer the questions using verb *to be*. Use short answers.

a) Are elephants gray and heavy?

....

b) Are you in school now?

....

c) Is your mother tall?

....

d) Is your schoolbag black?

....

e) Is today Friday?

....

REVIEW → The Picnic

1 Complete the sentences with *this*, *that*, *these* or *those*.

a) .... apples are fresh and delicious.

b) .... is my twin sister, Alana.

c) .... are beautiful stars.

d) .... is my dog Spencer.

2 Look at the pictures and write the season of the year.

a)
....

b)
....

c)
....

d)
....

3 Read the sentences and complete with *has* or *have*.

a) My sister .... a yellow and blue schoolbag.

b) Chris .... a cool new computer game.

c) I .... a school picnic next Monday.

d) Grandma and grandpa .... a new house.

REVIEW → Are You Ready?

1 What time is it? Write the time in full.

a)

It's ....

b)

It's ....

c)

It's ....

d)

It's ....

2 Read Randy's routine and fill in the blanks. Use the words from the box.

| have lunch   do the homework   walk the dog   take a shower |
| get up   get dressed   go to sleep   brush my teeth   have breakfast |

Hello, my name is Randy. I'm 10 years old and this is my daily routine.

I .... at 7 o'clock in the morning to go to school.

First, I ...., then I ....

Usually I .... with my mom and my brother Todd.
We like to have toast, butter, coffee and milk, and some fruit. Then

I .... and go to school.

My classes start at 8:30 a.m., and by 12:30 p.m.

I .... at school. Next I have

two more classes in the afternoon. School finishes at

3:30 p.m. I go back home, ... ,

have a snack and ....

At 7:30 p.m. I have dinner with my family. Then I watch cartoons on TV and at

10:00 p.m. I ....

REVIEW → The E-Generation

1 Read and match.

a) play

b) chat

c) listen

d) pay

e) drive

f) do

g) have

h) go

□ homework

□ to parties

□ a job or a cell phone

□ video game

□ on the internet

□ to music

□ the bills

□ a car

2 Now write sentences using the verbs from activity 1.

a) ....

b) ....

c) ....

d) ....

e) ....

f) ....

g) ....

h) ....

1 Read about Simon and Martha. Then complete the sentences with the correct verbs.

	run	dance	sing	draw
Simon	yes	no	yes	yes
Martha	no	yes	no	yes

a) Martha and Simon ....

b) Martha ....

c) Simon .... and ....

d) Martha ....

e) Martha ....

f) Simon ....

2 Now write two things you *can* or *can't do*.

a) ....

b) ....

REVIEW ⇒ Help the Planet!

1 Look at the pictures and answer the questions.

a) Is Paul washing his hands?

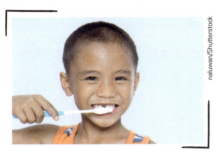

....

....

b) What are you doing, kids?

....

....

to reduce pollution.

c) Are you dancing?

....

....

d) Are they watching videos?

....

....

....

LET'S PLAY! ⇒ What Is Your Favorite Subject?

1 Complete with the missing numbers. Then write them in full.

12 + ... = 21	...... + 2 = 62	52 − ...... = 47	20 + ... = 30	2 x 40 = ...
....	....		....	....
...... x 15 = 45	20 : ...... = 10	...... − 9 = 91	...... x 25 = 100	...... : 3 = 10
....	....	....	....	....
2 x 35 = ...	...... + 38 = 57	...... : 2 = 4	25 − ...... = 11	21 + 8 = ...
....				

2 Guess the number sequence and complete.

a) ...., twenty-two, twenty-three

b) sixty-two, seventy-two, ...

c) forty-six, ..., forty-two

d) ...., thirty-four, thirty-eight

e) seventy, ..., ninety

3 Unscramble the words in bold and write them.

a) When is the **calPyhsi tiEducaon** class? ....

b) Take a look at the new **eludehcs**. ....

c) The second class is **toHyisr**. ....

d) I prefer **Scceein aclss**. ....

e) I like **EglInshi**. ....

Banco de imagens

LET'S PLAY! ⇉ School Games

1 Choose the words from the box and play bingo.

scavenger hunt   three-legged race   egg race   musical chair
hangman   spelling bee   bingo   tug of war   dodgeball

Banco de imagens

LET'S PLAY! → A Birthday Party

1 Read the invitation card and answer the questions.

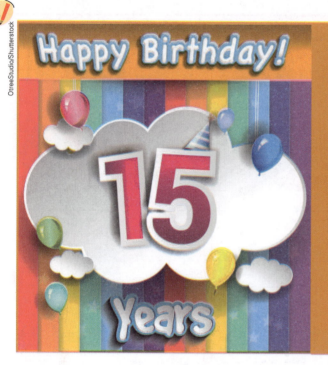

Happy Birthday!

15 Years

To: Justin

Come to my birthday party!

Date: Saturday, May 25th

Place: 60 High Street, Oldtown

Time: from 7.00 p.m. to 11.00 p.m.

Please reply by phone!

Telephone: 455-382

Mia

a) Who is having a birthday party? ....

b) When is the party? ....

c) What time is the party? ....

d) Where is the party? ....

e) Is Mia asking for a reply by phone? ....

f) What is Mia's telephone number? ....

g) How old is Mia? ....

h) Is Mia's birthday in March? ....

i) Is Mia's birthday on a Saturday? ....

j) Is Justin a guest? ....

LET'S PLAY! → The Picnic

1 Let's play a board game.

START

Say the name of the four seasons.

Pakkad Sah/Shutterstock

What's your favorite season? Why?

Move forward 1 square.

How many students are there in your classroom?

Complete with *this* or *that*.

.... is my friend Lisa.

KanKhem/Shutterstock

What day is today?

DEC 27

Jane Kelly/Shutterstock

Say the days of the week.

What's your favorite month? Why?

Complete with *have* or *has*.

He .... a car.

Complete with *this* or *these*.

.... are my students.

Artistico/ Shutterstock

Complete with *have* or *has*.

I .... a big family.

When is your birthday?

Go back two squares.

How old are you?

Say 5 picnic foods.

Sylfida/Shutterstock

FINISH

LET'S PLAY! → Are You Ready?

1 Circle 6 actions and write them next to the pictures.

G	E	T	*	U	P	T	K
V	T	K	P	A	S	A	Q
H	Y	L	O	E	D	K	A
A	U	X	U	D	O	E	U
V	G	E	T	T	E	Ç	E
E	O	B	Y	C	O	M	B

a) .... a shower.

b) .... your breakfast.

c) .... It's time to play soccer.

d) .... your homework, then you can play.

e) .... your hair before eating your breakfast.

f) .... dressed to go to the movies.

LET'S PLAY! → The E-Generation

1 Write 6 actions using the letters from the box. Then match the actions to the pictures.

I S T D E X B R A W L N U P Y

a) .... d ....   **b)** .... t ....

c) .... l ....   **d)** .... s ....

e) .... p ....   **f)** .... u ....

Olga1818/Shutterstock

ann13131313/Shutterstock

Ildar Galeev/Shutterstock

Pogorelova Olga/Shutterstock

Vasilyeva Larisa/Shutterstock

Iconic Bestiary/Shutterstock

LET'S PLAY! → Can You Ride a Bike?

1 Talk to your classmates. Then write what these people are doing.

	A	B	C	D
1	Nova II/Shutterstock	MP2021/Shutterstock	mijatmijatovic/Shutterstock	grynold/Shutterstock
2		Oleg_Yakovlev/Shutterstock	Snap2Art/Shutterstock / Kaimen/Shutterstock	Black creator 24/Shutterstock

LET'S PLAY! ⤳ Help the Planet!

1 Use the words from the box to complete the sentences.

| reduce | reuse | turn off | recycle | plant | use | save |

a) .... trees to clean the air from pollution.

b) .... the light when you are not in the room.

c) .... clothes and donate the ones you do not use anymore.

d) .... cloth bags when you go shopping.

e) .... water to help preserve the life on the planet.

f) .... plastic, old notebooks, magazines, newspapers and cans.

g) .... the amount of garbage you throw away.

AUDIO TRANSCRIPT

Track 3

zero, one, two, three, four, five, six, seven, eight, nine, ten, eleven, twelve, thirteen, fourteen, fifteen, sixteen, seventeen, eighteen, nineteen, twenty, thirty, forty, fifty, sixty, seventy, eighty, ninety, one hundred

Track 19

Sebastian: Hi, Julia! How are you?

Julia: Hello, Sebastian. I'm fine, thanks. And you?

Sebastian: I'm fine, thanks.

Julia: What is your favorite season of the year?

Sebastian: It is summer.

Julia: Why?

Sebastian: Because I like the beach. Would you like to go to the beach with me and my family next weekend?

Julia: Yes, I would love to go to the beach.

Track 20

Mom: Let's make our picnic list, Bob.

Bob: OK, mom. We need some fruit, cookies, sandwiches and orange juice.

Mom: That's perfect! Let's go to the supermarket.

Bob: Yeah! Let me grab the picnic list.

Track 25

a) Comb your hair, Joana.

b) Brush your teeth, Peter.

c) Go to sleep, Bobby.

d) Take a shower, Monica.

Track 30

1. They play video game.

2. She works in an office.

3. He draws lots of animals.

4. Susan texts her friends.

5. These teenagers love to go to parties.

6. She pays the supermarket bill.

7. He drives to work every day.

8. My cousin listens to music.

Track 35

Narrator:

Katie can play the electric guitar well.

Jeff can't dance.

Susan can't cook dinner because she doesn't like to cook.

John can ride his BMS bike. He is good at it.

Alan can play soccer. He plays every day after school.

Track 39

a) My friends are planting a tree.

b) John is riding his bike to work.

c) My mom is using a cloth bag for shopping.

d) The kids are drinking water because it is hot.

GLOSSARY

A

a: um, uma
about: sobre, acerca de
above: acima
according to: de acordo com
act out: atuar, encenar
action: ação
actor: ator, atriz
add: adicionar, somar
address: endereço
afraid of: temer; ter medo de
after: depois de, após
afternoon: tarde
again: de novo, novamente
age: idade
ahead: em frente
aloud: em voz alta
all: todos
alone: sozinho(a)
alphabet letter: letra do alfabeto
also: também
always: sempre,
a.m.: antes do meio-dia (*ante meridiem*)
am: sou; estou
amazing: incrível, maravilhoso
an: um, uma
and: e
angry: bravo, irritado
announce: anunciar
answer: resposta; responder
ant: formiga
anything: nada; algo
apple: maçã
April: abril
are: são; estão
around: ao redor de
arrive: chegar
Art: Arte (disciplina)
article: artigo
ask: perguntar; pedir

at: no, na, para
at home: em casa
August: agosto
aunt: tia
away: para longe
awesome: incrível, fantástico

B

baby: bebê
baby brother: irmão caçula
back: atrás; para trás
bad behavior: mau comportamento
bake: assar
balance: equilíbrio
balloon: balão, bexiga
barbecue wooden stick: palito de churrasco
basket: cesta
bathroom: banheiro
be careful: ter cuidado
be good at: ser bom em (alguma coisa)
be green: ser verde, preservar o meio ambiente
be respectful: ser respeitoso
be sad: estar triste
be tired: estar cansado(a)
be well: estar bem, sentir--se bem
beach: praia
beanbag: saquinho com feijões ou areia dentro
beautiful: bonito(a)
because: porque
become: tornar-se
bed: cama
bedroom: quarto
behind: atrás de
below: abaixo de, embaixo de
best: melhor
best friend: melhor amigo(a)

better: melhor
between: entre
bicycle: bicicleta
big: grande
bill: conta, fatura, boleto
bird: pássaro
birthday: aniversário
black: preto(a)
blank: lacuna
blanket: cobertor
bloom: florescer
blow out: apagar (vela)
blue: azul
board game: jogo de tabuleiro
body: corpo humano
bomb: bomba
bone: osso
book: livro
bookshelf: prateleira, estante de livros
border: borda
bottle: garrafa
bottle cap: tampinha de garrafa
box: caixa, quadro
bread: pão
breakfast: café da manhã
bring: trazer
brother: irmão
brown: marrom
brush teeth: escovar os dentes
bush: arbusto
busy: ocupado(a)
but: mas
butter: manteiga
buy: comprar
bye-bye: tchau; até logo

C

cake: bolo
can: poder, conseguir
Canadian: canadense
candle: vela
candy: bala, guloseimas

captions: legendas
card: cartão
cardboard: cartolina; papelão
carrot cake: bolo de cenoura
cartoon: desenho animado
cartoonist: cartunista
cat: gato(a)
celebrate: celebrar, comemorar
cell phone: telefone celular
cereal: grãos, cereal
chair: cadeira
chalk: giz (de lousa)
chart: tabela, quadro
cheat: trapacear
chicken wrap: sanduíche embrulhado de frango
child: criança
childhood: infância
children: crianças
choice: escolha
choose: escolher
Christmas: Natal
city: cidade
class schedule: grade de horário escolar
classes: aulas
classmate: colega de turma
classroom: sala de aula
clean: limpar
climb: subir, escalar
clock hand: ponteiro de relógio
close: fechar
cloth bag: sacola de tecido
clues: dicas
collar: coleira
comb hair: pentear cabelo
come: vir
comic strip: tirinha
computer: computador
contest: concurso, competição

cook: cozinhar
cookies: biscoitos
cool: legal, bacana
copy: copiar
country: país
countryside: campo
cousin: primo(a)
curtains: cortinas
cut: cortar

D

dad: papai
daily routine: rotina diária
dairy: laticínios, derivados do leite
dance: dançar
date: data
days of the week: dias da semana
December: dezembro
definition: definição
delicious: delicioso, gostoso
desk: carteira escolar
dictionary entry: verbete de dicionário
dinner: jantar
do: fazer
do homework: fazer o dever de casa
dog: cachorro
don't mind: não se preocupe
draw: desenhar
dress: vestir-se; vestido
drink: beber; bebida
drive: dirigir

E

each: cada
early: cedo
eat: comer
E-generation: geração tecnológica
egg race: corrida do ovo na colher
eighth: oitavo

eighteenth: décimo oitavo
elder: ancião, anciã
eleventh: décimo primeiro
energy: energia (elétrica)
engineer: engenheiro(a)
English: Língua Inglesa (disciplina)
enjoy: divertir-se
environment: meio ambiente
equality: igualdade
equals to: igual a
eraser: borracha escolar
evening: (final de) tarde, noite
every: cada, todo
every day: todo dia
everyone: todos
excitement: entusiasmo
excuse: desculpar
exercise: exercitar-se
explain: explicar
eyes: olhos

F

fact: fato
fair play: jogo limpo
fall: outono; cair
family: família
fast: rápido(a)
fat: gordo, obeso; gordura
father: pai
faucet: torneira
favorite: favorito, predileto
fear: medo
February: fevereiro
feel good: sentir-se bem
feeling: sentimento; sentir
feet: pés
fever: febre
find: achar, encontrar
fifteenth: décimo quinto
fifth: quinto
fill in: preencher, completar
find: achar, encontrar
fine: bem; bom
first: primeiro

floor: chão, piso
flower: flor
flyer: folheto publicitário
food: comida, alimento(s)
for: para
forget: esquecer
forty: quarenta
fourteenth: décimo quarto
fourth: quarto
frame: moldura
free: livre
French: francês, francesa
French fries: batatas fritas
fresh air: ar fresco
Friday: sexta-feira
friend: amigo(a)
friendly: amigável
from: de
fruit: fruta
fruit salad: salada de frutas
full: cheio
fun: divertir-se; diversão
funny: engraçado(a)

G

game: jogo, brincadeira
game rules: regras do jogo
game week: semana de jogos
gap: lacuna
garbage: lixo
garbage bin: lixeira coletiva
garden: jardim
gasoline (gas): gasolina
generate: gerar, criar
Geography: Geografia (disciplina)
get: chegar
get a job: arrumar emprego, trabalho
get dressed: aprontar-se, vestir-se
get rest: descansar
get up: levantar-se
gift: presente

girl: menina, garota
give: dar
glad to meet: feliz em conhecer
glass: vidro
glue: colar; cola
go: ir
go back 1 square: voltar uma casa no jogo
go dance: ir dançar
go on: continuar
go round: girar (ao redor de algo)
go shopping: ir às compras
go to school: ir à escola
go to sleep: ir dormir
go to parties: ir a festas
good: bom; boa
good afternoon: boa tarde
good evening: boa noite
good habits: bons hábitos
good morning: bom dia
good night: boa noite
grains: grãos, cereais
grandma: vovó
grandpa: vovô
grapes: uvas
gray: cinza (cor)
great: grande; ótimo
green: verde (cor)
greetings: saudações, cumprimentos
grid: matriz, grade
ground: chão
grow up: crescer
grown-up: adulto
guess: adivinhar
guessing game: jogo de adivinhas
guest: convidado(a)
guide: guia
guitar: violão

H

habit: costume; hábito
hair: cabelo; pelo
half: metade

hangman: jogo da forca
happy: feliz
hat: chapéu
have: ter
have breakfast: tomar café da manhã
have dinner: jantar
have fun: divertir-se
have lunch: almoçar
health: saúde
healthy: saudável
heavy: pesado
helmet: capacete
help: ajudar; ajuda
helpful: prestativo
high-tech: de alta tecnologia
History: História (disciplina)
home: casa; lar
homework: tarefa de casa
hot: quente
house: casa
how: como
How are you?: Como você está?
How many...?: Quanto...?, Quanta...?
How often...?: Com que frequência...?
hundred: centena
hungry: com fome, faminto
Hurray!: Hurra!
Hurry up!: apressar-se, pressa

I

I: eu
I'll be there!: Eu estarei lá!
I'm: eu sou; eu estou
I would love to: Eu adoraria...
implement: implementar
in: em; dentro
in case of: em caso de
in full: por extenso
in pairs: em duplas
insect: inseto
inside: dentro de

instruction: instrução
integrity: integridade
interview: entrevista; entrevistar
invitation: convite
is: é; está

J

January: janeiro
jealousy: ciúmes; inveja
job: trabalho, emprego
join: juntar-se
juicy: suculento
July: julho
jump: pular, saltar
June: junho
junk food: comida calórica e pouco nutritiva

K

key words: palavras--chave
kid: criança
kitchen: cozinha
know: saber, conhecer
knowledge: conhecimento

L

late: tarde
laugh: risada, gargalhada
lazy: preguiçoso(a)
leave: deixar, sair
leaves: folhas (de plantas)
lemonade: limonada
less: menos
Let me see!: Deixe-me ver!
Let's go!: Vamos!
letter: carta; letra
life: vida
light: luz
like: gostar; como
list: lista; listar
listen: escutar, ouvir
litter: lixo
live: viver, habitar
long: longo, comprido
look: olhar
lose: perder
lots of: muitos(as)

love: amor; amar, adorar
lunch: almoço
lyrics: letra de música

M

magazine: revista
make: fazer
make sure: certifique-se de que
man: homem
many: muitos
March: março
match: ligar, relacionar
Math: Matemática (disciplina)
Math class: aula de Matemática
May: maio
me: me, mim
meal: comida, refeição
meaning of: significado (de)
measure: medir
meat: carne
meet: conhecer
meeting: reunião
midday: meio-dia
midnight: meia-noite
milk: leite
mind: mente
minus: sinal de subtração
miss a turn: perder a vez no jogo
missing: faltando, que falta
mix: misturar
mom: mamãe
Monday: segunda-feira
month: mês
morning: manhã
Mother's Day: Dia das Mães
mouse: *mouse* de computador
mouse pad: tapete de *mouse*
move: mover; mudar
move forward: mover adiante
mulberry: amoreira

musical chair game: jogo das cadeiras
my: meu, minha

N

name: nome
nature: natureza
naughty: travesso, levado
need: precisar, necessitar
never: nunca
new: novo(a)
newspaper: jornal
next to: ao lado de
night: noite
nineteenth: décimo nono
ninth: nono
note: bilhete, nota
November: novembro
now: agora
number: número; numerar

O

obey: obedecer
o'clock: hora exata
October: outubro
offer: oferecer
old: velho(a)
on: em, sobre, no, na
open: abrir; aberto(a)
open gift: abrir presente, desembrulhar
opposite: oposto, contrário de
orange juice: suco de laranja
order: ordem, sequência
ordinal number: numeral ordinal
other: outro(a)
our: nosso(s), nossa(s)
out: fora; para fora
outside: fora, do lado de fora
own: próprio

P

package: pacote, embalagem
page: página
parent: pai, mãe ou responsável

park: parque
party: festa
pay: pagar
peach: pêssego
pebble: pedra, pedrinha
pedal: pedal; pedalar
peel: descascar
people: pessoas
Physical Education (P.E.): Educação Física (disciplina)
picnic: piquenique
picture: figura, imagem, foto
pie: torta
piece: pedaço
place: local, lugar
planet: planeta
plastic bottle: garrafa de plástico
play: brincar; jogar; tocar
play fair: jogar limpo
play soccer: jogar futebol
please: por favor
plus: sinal de adição
p.m.: depois do meio-dia, à tarde
pollution: poluição
Portuguese: Língua Portuguesa (disciplina)
poster: cartaz, pôster
potato chips: batatas fritas
practice: prática; praticar
practitioner of medicine: médico(a)
prefer: preferir
pretty: bonito(a)
princess: princesa
provide: dar, proporcionar
push: empurrar, impulsionar
put: pôr, colocar
put on: vestir, colocar

Q

question: pergunta; perguntar
quick: rápido(a)

quickly: rapidamente
quiz: questionário

R

reach: alcançar, chegar
read: ler
recipe: receita
recycle: reciclar
red: vermelho(a)
reduce: reduzir, diminuir
remember: lembrar, recordar
resource: recurso
respect: respeito; respeitar
respectful: respeitoso(a)
rest: descansar
reusable: reutilizável
reuse: reutilizar, reusar
ride (a car): dirigir (carro)
ride a bike: andar de bicicleta
road: rua, estrada
routine: rotina
rule: regra
run: correr
run fast: correr rápido

S

sad: triste
sandwich: sanduíche
Saturday: sábado
save: economizar; salvar
say: dizer
scavenger hunt: caça ao tesouro
schedule: horário; programação
school: escola
schoolbag: mochila escolar
school subject: disciplina escolar
Science: Ciências (disciplina)
scissors: tesoura
scrap: pedaço, sucata
scrapbook: álbum de recortes
search: procurar, pesquisar

season: estação do ano
second: segundo
see: ver
see you: te vejo lá
send: enviar
September: setembro
seventh: sétimo
seventeenth: décimo sétimo
share: compartilhar, dividir
shop: fazer compras
short: baixo(a); curto(a)
shower: banho, ducha
sick: doente
sincerely: sinceramente
sing: cantar
singer: cantor(a)
sister: irmã
sit down: sentar-se
sixth: sexto
sixteenth: décimo sexto
skate: andar de patins
skip: ir pulando, saltar
sleep: dormir
slogan: lema, mote
small: pequeno(a)
snack: lanche, petisco
sneakers: tênis (calçado)
social life: vida social
solidarity: solidariedade
some: algum, alguns
someone: alguém
sorry: desculpe(-me)
spell: soletrar
spelling bee contest: competição de soletrar palavras
spinach pie: torta de espinafre
sport: esporte
spring: primavera
square: casa do jogo, quadrado
stand: ficar em pé
start: começar
step: passo, etapa
stick: colar; palito de churrasco
subject: assunto, tema, disciplina escolar

summer: verão
sun: Sol
Sunday: domingo
sure: claro, com certeza
surf the internet: navegar na internet
sustainability: sustentabilidade
sustainable: sustentável
sweets: doces
swim: nadar
switch off: desligar
symbol: símbolo

T

table: mesa
tail: rabo
take a shower: tomar banho
take pictures: fotografar, tirar fotos
tall: alto(a)
teacher: professor(a)
teenager: adolescente
teeth: dentes
tenth: décimo
text: texto; enviar mensagem de texto
thank you: obrigado (a você)
that: aquele, aquela, aquilo
the: o, a, os, as
the best: o melhor
their: deles, delas
them: os, as
there: lá
there to be: haver, existir
these: estes, estas
thin: magro(a)
think: pensar
third: terceiro
this: este, esta, isto
thirteenth: décimo terceiro
thirtieth: trigésimo
three-legged race: corrida de três pernas
Thursday: quinta-feira
time: tempo, hora

to: para
toast: torrada
today: hoje
tolerance: tolerância
tonight: esta noite
too: muito; também
too early: muito cedo
touch: contato, tocar
tourism: turismo
transportation: transporte
trash: lixo
travel: viajar
tree: árvore
true: verdadeiro
Tuesday: terça-feira
tug of war: cabo de guerra
tuna sandwich: sanduíche de atum
turn: vez (no jogo)
turn off: desligar, apagar
turn on: ligar
twelfth: décimo segundo
twentieth: vigésimo
twenty-first: vigésimo primeiro
twenty-fourth: vigésimo quarto
twenty-second: vigésimo segundo
twenty-third: vigésimo terceiro
twin sister: irmã gêmea

U

ugly: feio(a)
under: sob, embaixo de
understand: entender, compreender
unhealthy: não saudável
unscramble: desembaralhar
usually: normalmente, geralmente

V

variety: variedade
vegetables: legumes, verduras
veggies: vegetais
very: muito

violence: violência
visit: visitar

W

wait: esperar
wake up: despertar, acordar
walk: andar, caminhar
want: querer
watch TV: assistir à televisão
water: água
watermelon: melancia
wear: vestir; usar
Wednesday: quarta-feira
week: semana
welcome: bem-vindo
well: bem
what: que, qual
What time is it?: Que horas são?
wheel: roda
when: quando
where: onde
which: que, qual
white: branco(a)
white cardboard: cartolina branca
who: quem
why: por que, por quê
win: ganhar
winter: inverno
witch: bruxa
wonderful: maravilhoso
word: palavra
work: trabalho; trabalhar
world: mundo
write: escrever

Y

yard: jardim
year: ano
yellow: amarelo(a)
yes: sim
your: seu(s), sua(s)
yourself: você mesmo(a), si mesmo

SUGGESTIONS FOR STUDENTS

Books

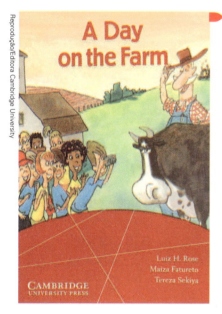

Luiz H. Rose, Maiza Fatureto e Tereza Sekiya. **A Day on the Farm**. Cambridge University Press, 2007.

Três professores de inglês decidem organizar um dia de atividades em uma fazenda para os alunos praticarem o idioma em um contexto real e diferente. Ao final dessa vivência, os alunos aprendem muito mais do que inglês; aprendem uma verdadeira lição de vida.

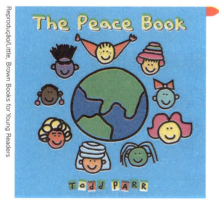

Todd Parr. **The Peace Book**. Little Brown for Young Readers, 2005.

Esse livro traz mensagens positivas de paz para crianças desta faixa etária. O livro é ricamente ilustrado com cores fortes e brilhantes e com a delicadeza de cenas simples, sendo perfeito para jovens leitores. A mensagem trazida por essa obra é atemporal sobre a importância da amizade, do carinho e da aceitação.

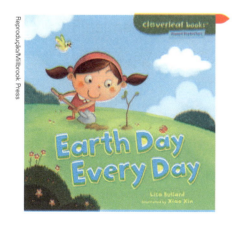

Lisa Bullard. **Earth Day Every Day.** Série Cloverleaf Books. Millbrook Press TM, 2011.

Nesse livro encontramos sugestões de como podemos ajudar o planeta Terra. A personagem Trina planta árvores com a ajuda dos colegas de turma dela. Ela decide formar um clube chamado Earth Day Club. Descubra pequenas coisas que você pode fazer diariamente para salvar o planeta.

● Sites

www.gamestolearnenglish.com/

Esse *site* traz uma grande variedade de jogos para estimular a aquisição de vocabulário novo e praticar estruturas de gramática por meio de jogos educativos e oferece uma forma divertida e prazerosa para dinamizar a aula.

https://www.cbc.ca/kidscbc2/games

O *site* CBC KIDS tem como objetivo levar às crianças vídeos e jogos educacionais simples que oferecem prática de vocabulário e de estruturas gramaticais de forma prazerosa e lúdica.

https://pt.bab.la/dicionario/ingles-portugues

O dicionário bab.la *on-line* oferece a tradução de palavras e expressões de inglês para o português e vice-versa, além de apresentar os sinônimos das palavras. Os vocábulos e expressões são atualizados constantemente por um grupo de linguistas.

BIBLIOGRAPHY

ALMEIDA FILHO, J. C. P. *Dimensões comunicativas no ensino de línguas*. 2. ed. Campinas: Pontes, 2000.

BRASIL. Base Nacional Comum Curricular (BNCC). Brasília, DF: MEC, 2018. Disponível em: <http://basenacionalcomum.mec.gov.br/>. Acesso em: 26 set. 2019.

CELANI, M. A. A. *Ensino de segunda língua*: redescobrindo as origens. São Paulo: Educ, 1997.

HARMER, J. *The Practice of English Language Teaching*. 4. ed. London: Pearson Longman, 2007.

MOITA LOPES, L. P. A nova ordem mundial, os Parâmetros Curriculares Nacionais e o ensino de inglês no Brasil. A base intelectual para uma ação política. In: BARBARA, L.; RAMOS, R. de C. G. *Reflexão e ações no ensino-aprendizagem de línguas*. São Paulo: Mercado de Letras, 2003.

VYGOTSKY, L. S. *A formação social da mente*: o desenvolvimento dos processos psicológicos superiores. São Paulo: Martins Fontes, 1991.

FINISH

START

CARDS

What is your name?

My name is _____.

How are you?

I'm fine, thanks.

Can you swim?

Yes, I can. / No, I can't.

What time is it?

It's _____.

How old are you?

I'm _____ years old.

Where are you?

I'm at _____ .

How many boys are there in your classroom?

There are _____ .

How many girls are there in your classroom?

There are _____ .

What is this?

(Apontar para um lápis.)

It is a pencil.

What is this?

(Apontar para um livro.)

It is a book.

What color is it?
(Apontar para a cor
verde no tabuleiro.)

It's green.

What is the first month
of the year?

It's January.

Say the next day of
the week:
Sunday, Monday, Tuesday...

Wednesday

Say the next ordinal number:
first, second, third...

fourth

What color is it?
(Apontar para a cor
amarela no tabuleiro.)

It's yellow.

What is the fifth month
of the year?

It's May.

Say the next month of
the year:
January, February, March...

April

Say the next number:
twenty, thirty, forty...

fifty

STICKERS

🍅 **Lesson 1 — What Is Your Favorite Subject?**

Monkey Business Images/Shutterstock

James Steidl/Shutterstock

Juice Images/Adobe Fotolia/Glow Images

Mauritius Images/Alamy/Fotoarena

Monkey Business Images/Shutterstock

Monkey Business Images/Shutterstock

AVAVA/Shutterstock

Age Fotostock/Easypix Brasil

🍂 Lesson 4 — The Picnic

Fotos: Mihai_Andritoiu/Shutterstock

🍂 Lesson 8 — Help the Planet!

Robert Kneschke/Shutterstock

Africa Studio/Shutterstock

Rawpixel.com/Shutterstock

Halfpoint/Shutterstock

5º ANO

Treasure Hunt

Eliete Canesi Morino

Rita Brugin de Faria

Aluno: ....

Escola: .... Turma: ....

Editora Scipione

TREASURE HUNT
INSTRUCTIONS
1. The game includes four tasks.
2. Do the tasks in groups.
3. The group that does all the tasks first wins the game.
The prize are tickets for a water park.

TASKS

1. Take a picture of something moving fast.
2. Write the name of a green insect.
3. Take a picture of a big rock.
4. Find and describe a nest.